Rethink Productivity by Paul O'Mahony

Design by Luke Bunting
Research by Paul O'Mahony
© Copyright 2021 Paul O'Mahony

Printed in Peterborough, Cambridgeshire, UK
ISBN: 978-1-914951-00-8

Published by Rethink Academy Ltd
Unit 107, Moat House, 54 Bloomfield Avenue,
Belfast, Ireland, BT5 5AD

www.RethinkTimeManagement.com/productivity
www.RethinkTimeManagement.com/course
www.RethinkPlanner.com/reorder
www.RethinkBooks.club

Paul O'Mahony

Contents

1.0 Introduction
Congratulations!

I am very excited for you right now, and I want to be the first to congratulate you. Little do you know, but by opening this *RETHINK! Planner*, you have taken the very first step in empowering yourself to create a life in which you will:

- Be less stressed

- Have clear priorities

- Have a real sense of control

- Be set up for success in all areas

- Set and hit all your targets

- Get ahead rather than fall behind

- Dramatically reduce your sense of overwhelm

- Free your day up to spend your time on things you love to do

- Be at least five to ten times more productive each day

- Be and feel much healthier, both physically and mentally

- Finally end your endless battle with time!

- … And have fun while doing it

You may think these are grand claims to make right from the off. But if anything, I am being conservative! This planner can and will turn your life around completely, dramatically and quickly.

Imagine for a moment a life that you feel you are living by design rather than in constant reactionary mode.

Imagine a world where to-do lists can become a thing of the past, and where you feel in control of the amazing journey we call life!

Imagine feeling in a state of almost effortless flow, where you know how to set and hit goals as if you had known how all your life.

No longer does any of this need to be a part of your imagination; it is about to become very real – and fast.

Welcome to the *RETHINK! Planner*

This planner is the culmination of reading over a hundred different books on the topics of personal development and time management, written by incredible experts over the past hundred years or more.

As I read each book, I went through the painstaking task of testing out every theory they shared, using myself as the guinea pig to find the elements that worked best. I discarded the rest.

While this publication is a "planner", it really is so much more, as you are about to discover. I will start by sharing some of my own successes to help inspire you and show you the truly life-changing power of this planner. At the time of writing, this planner has been directly responsible for helping me:

- Jog every day for 1,492 days in a row

- Cut sugar out of my diet for 1,050 days (excluding fruit, vegetables and alcohol!)

- Eat no bread for 704 days

- Eat no cheese for 704 days

- Include greens in my diet for 623 days

- Include probiotics in my diet for 623 days

- Do "energy clearing" daily for 520 days (more information available on page 153 of the *RETHINK! Planner* section)

- Lift weights daily for 230 days

- Drink Alkaline Iodised Water daily for 180 days (more information available on page 152 of the *RETHINK! Planner* section)

- Have a cold shower for 95 days

By the time you are reading this, each of these streaks will have increased significantly. As you can probably guess, these behaviours have resulted in simply incredible differences in my life – and the lives of those closest to me.

At one point or another, I had failed at or completely given up on ever being able to do every single one of these activities. These were things "other people" could do, but not me. That was before the *RETHINK! Planner*. ☺

Thanks to this planner, I have dropped from 25% body fat to 8%, and I have earned tens of millions of dollars through my businesses. But best of all, I have absolute certainty when it comes to setting and achieving goals, and I have peace of mind knowing I have this "secret weapon" to use at any time. I would not give up this planner for anything!

Since embarking on this journey of using variations of a planner in 2000, I have now created what I believe to be the most effective tool in the industry – and I should know, as I have read, used and tested almost everything out there! I have stood on the shoulders of giants to bring you the best approaches there are!

This planner has been updated multiple times and gone through hundreds of iterations. I only kept the most effective and powerful elements to create the planner you have in your hands right now. This planner has been used by literally tens of thousands of my clients in more than 150 countries, and the reports about how their lives have changed are truly remarkable.

Finally, your time has come to create your very own success story, starting today. I hope you are as excited to get stuck in as I am to be with you at the very start of this incredibly inspiring and empowering journey you are about to take. Let's get started!

2.0 What is "RETHINK!"?

In this section, I would like to explain to you the thought process behind the word "RETHINK!" and why it is core to the success of your planner.

Yes, I certainly do wish for you to rethink how planners are used and how impactful they can be for you, but there is more to this planner than meets the eye...

In case you are not aware, there is a best-seller companion book to this *RETHINK! Planner* called *Rethink Time Management* – G.O.D.'s Guide to Heaven on Earth (more information available on page 149). It explains in depth how to use the planner and gets into detail on the topics included in the planner. It also provides the background to each segment of this planner, explaining why each one has ended up in here. This planner is not so much about the theory of being effective and becoming a time management ninja, but rather the practical application of the theory. If you do wish to dive in deeper to the origins of each part of the planner, then I advise you to either get your hands on a physical or digital copy or listen to the audio version on Audible. However, you don't need to read *Rethink Time Management* to use this planner, as I will provide detailed instructions here for getting start right away.

Have you ever wondered why you find some things easy to do, and other things a real struggle? Have you noticed that there are some activities that you would jump out of bed to do first thing in the morning, and never need to be reminded of, while others you find literally any excuse to avoid or seem to conveniently forget?

Unfortunately, it is often those things that we would rather not do that end up being the most important tasks of all, as we constantly procrastinate until they pile up ready to fall over. As the seemingly ever-growing to-do list builds quickly over time, it can add high levels of unnecessary stress to our lives. If we are honest with ourselves, most of us often think of our to-do list as our to-avoid list – if the task were easy or enjoyable to do, it would already be done!

This is why having a daily planner is so important. It serves multiple purposes, one being that it is a crucial accountability tool. It ensures you know how to prioritise your tasks for the day ahead and helps you reduce lists rather than adding to them.

When it comes to your natural sense of prioritising your tasks right now, much of this process relates to the elements that you value most in life. Most people not only don't know what their values are, but unfortunately, they do not understand how detrimental the impact of not knowing their values can be on both their physical and mental well-being.

This can lead to a feeling of overwhelm and stress on a regular basis when we have no true way of knowing and prioritizing what we must or should be doing. As a result, we end up responding to those shouting the loudest for our attention. This inevitably leads to a general sense of unease with oneself. Is it any wonder that the top four leading causes of death are stress-related? This truly can be a matter of life or death.

The objective of this planner is not to help you find your values, as this is already addressed in the *Rethink Time Management* companion book. Instead, it allows you to not only set clear priorities but to also hold yourself accountable to accomplish these tasks.

To keep this as easy and practical as possible, we need to reduce the overwhelm one can associate with the term "life". Too often it feels like one big jumble of never-ending actions and activities. One of the best ways

I have found to resolve this problem is to categorize "life" into separate components. For the purposes of this planner, I divide "life" into eight areas, which conveniently fit the word "*RETHINK!*"

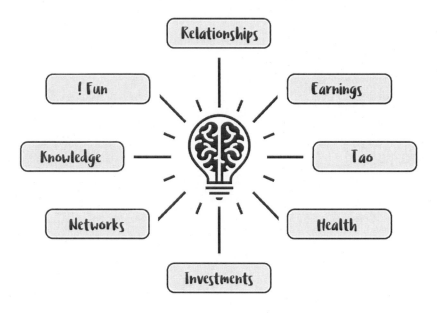

Figure 2.1 The 8 RETHINK! Areas of Life

Categorising your life into the eight areas shown here can immediately bring a sense of calm, as you start to appreciate that life doesn't need to be one big busy mess. As you go through life, each of these eight areas will have varying degrees of importance to you. However, none of these areas can be completely ignored, or you will end up paying the consequences later. Throughout the *RETHINK! Planner*, these eight areas are fundamental to bringing shape and control to your day. It is important to set goals in all eight areas, no matter how trivial, to maintain some form of blend or balance in your life.

What does each of these eight *RETHINK!* areas mean?...

RELATIONSHIPS:

This is one of the easiest areas to understand and one of the most popular of all areas, the focus being on your family and immediate circle of friends. This begins with your immediate family unit of parents and children, as well as siblings and extended family. It reaches beyond family to include the friends you associate with the most. Since these are the people that you spend the most time with, they impact on your belief systems and earnings more than anyone else in your life.

EARNINGS:

This area is about your ability to earn money by exchanging your time for money. In essence, this means having a job, being self-employed or running a business where you are being paid directly in line with how many hours you work. It is the most common method for people to acquire money. The more experience you have and the more value you can provide to a company, generally the more you get paid per hour. The number of hours in the week that you work is your limiter in terms of earnings.

TAO:

Tao is a Chinese word that means the way, the path or the route. Tao is the underlying natural order of the universe. I use this word rather than "spirituality" because, firstly, there is no "S" in RETHINK! ☺ But secondly, and more importantly, because the word "spirituality" is often placed in the same box as "religion", which has quite different meanings for individuals based on their background and upbringing. Tao may be as simple as a meditation or ritual practice. In my case, I carry out an incredible daily energy clearing ritual as part of this (you can find out more on page 153 of the RETHINK! Planner section), and I couldn't imagine starting my day without it!

HEALTH:

This is where you direct your attention to your physical body, your fitness, your interest in your appearance, your weight, your clothing, your exercise routines, your eating habits and anything else that's related to how you look and feel.

INVESTMENTS:

In this area, the main focus is specifically how money itself is used to earn more money. It focuses on how to save, grow, invest, compound and use money effectively. It also involves having a good understanding of the systems related to finances, such as the economy, and basically anything related to growing money without you having to exchange your time for money. In time, it allows you to become financially free.

NETWORKS:

This area is about the extended range of people you know or impact beyond your immediate set of "relationships" with family and closest friends. It is made up of your network of slightly more distant acquaintances, including former classmates, business connections, associates, work colleagues and, on a grander scale, the networks you can access to influence and impact locally, nationally and globally.

KNOWLEDGE:

This area is associated with your mental growth. It is about working on improving the grey matter between your ears. Growth of your knowledge can be achieved through traditional education, books, courses, coaching, mentoring and through dedicating time, effort and focus on pursuits of your specialised knowledge.

! FUN:

Although working on the other seven areas may be fun for you from time to time, it is much more reassuring to plan fun activities into your schedule, to ensure they happen. The use of the planner should not feel like a chore or as though you are living in a military bootcamp! The goals and targets you choose will be inspiring to you. And you will use the fun area to plan in rewards and to ensure you make time to truly enjoy yourself.

Now that you understand each of the eight areas, you can shape what success might look like for you in each of them. To know what to prioritise and how to use your time effectively each day, you must first determine what you wish to achieve in each area.

Your Next Steps

In the exercises in the next five steps, you will go on a journey to discover what your ideal lifestyle looks like at some specific point in the future for you.

You will then subdivide your "dream day" into the eight categories of life and get more specific about outcomes.

Step 1:

You will determine the goals you wish to achieve by the end of this year in each of the eight areas: Relationships, Earnings, Tao, Health, Investments, Networks, Knowledge and Fun!

Step 2:

Write each of them in "SMARTER" format: Specific, Measurable, Achievable, Relevant, Timebound, Evaluated and Reviewed. See chapter 12.3.2 of *Rethink Time Management* for more information on this. An example could be: "I am exercising daily for a minimum of 15 minutes and have a resting heart rate of 55 bpm and body fat of 15% or less by 31st of December 2030 or sooner." Do this on a blank piece of paper repeatedly until you arrive at the final wording you are happy with. This is what you'll enter into the planner shortly.

Step 3:

Once you are clear on your year-end goals in all eight areas, you then break them down into quarterly goals across the year. Make your best estimate of where you need to be at the end of each quarter to hit your year-end goals. You will get better at this every single quarter that you use the planner. A full breakdown on how to set 1 to 15-year goals and then bring this back to quarterly, weekly and daily goals is available in Psalms 12 and 13 of *Rethink Time Management*.

Step 4:

Note the date and day you are starting to use the planner and move to the right week number and specific day in your *RETHINK! Planner*.

Step 5:

It's time to use the *RETHINK! Planner* ☺

3.0 How To Use Your *RETHINK! Planner*

In this section, you'll find out how to use the planner. You can use this section as a reference to return to if you ever need clarification on how to use any element of the *RETHINK! Planner*.

As I mentioned earlier, this is the one tool that I would not give up for anything, and now you are ready to unravel how you use this powerhouse of a tool!

Although using the planner is quite self-explanatory, with little prompts in each box and symbols identifying what time of day to use them, what follows is a more in-depth explanation of how to get the most out of the planner. I definitely recommend that you read it at least the very first time you use this planner.

I will start with an overview of the first four sections, which together make up your map of your annual, quarterly, monthly and weekly goal-setting tools.

The good news is that if you do this the first time you use the planner, you can then simply copy your 10-15 year, annual, monthly, quarterly and weekly goals over to the next planner.

In this first section called "My Dream Life", your first exercise is to carry out (what should be) a very enjoyable task! It involves setting aside some time to ask yourself a simple question: "What would I do with my day if a lack of money was not an issue?" This planner is purposely designed for you to fill in with a pen or pencil; I find it is a lot easier to write physically than to type when you are starting the process of thinking about things. A short pencil is much better than a long memory!

Allow approximately 20 to 30 minutes to complete the task. Just sit down and start writing. Don't take your pen or pencil off the page – keep writing solidly about what you want, what you would love to have, who you'd love to be, where you'd love to go and so on. It might take a bit of time to get into flow, but once you do, you might find that you get a little greedy and start writing down all kinds of things.

I recommend you include all eight areas of life that we went through earlier: Relationships, Earnings, Tao, Health, Investments, Networks, Knowledge and Fun. Be sure to include this last one – think about the really fun things you'd like to do.

If you're into sports, maybe you'd love to go to a Wimbledon final or go scuba diving, paragliding or parachuting. Maybe you'd rather go to the World Cup finals in football or rugby, or to the NBA, NHL or MLB finals, or even the Super Bowl! If, like me, you're into travel, let your imagination run wild. Set your sights on going to Hawaii, Fiji or Pilau, or think about visiting the Great Barrier Reef and the other the wonders of the world.

Whatever it is that you love, be sure to write it down. Include the big dreams and the little ones, and write down wishes that are in your immediate future as well as those that are a decade away. Keep writing, regardless of how unbelievable it might seem.

A few minutes in, you may start to say to yourself "God, this is stupid. This isn't going to do me any good." What I've found, however, is that the opposite is true. When you get into the exercise, you may find it starts to inspire and motivate you to picture what your life could be like. The dreams become a lot more believable once they're written down than they were floating around in your head.

Be imaginative, and don't limit yourself! The exercise doesn't need to be just for your dreams either; you can do it for your family's dreams as well. Do it for whoever and whatever drives you and inspires you. When you're writing, it's a good idea to write in the present tense, as though you already have the things you're dreaming about.

Don't stop until you feel you have left nothing out. If you're still writing and 45 minutes have elapsed, that's great. Just keep going. There's no need to stop, because the more you get written down, the more powerful the exercise is.

One important thing to remember is that no one else is going to see this but you. You won't be sharing this with anybody, unless you want to share it with your life partner who supports you, for example. If you were to share this with the wrong person, they might think you're a bit crazy, or make a comment that knocks your confidence, possibly without intending to. If this happens, remember that it's most likely because they're scared of the possibility that you could achieve this dream life and they may not be part of your future plans.

You might be cringing right now at the prospect of dreaming. I get it – years ago, I was someone who laughed at the whole idea of setting goals! But if you are struggling with your time, I can guarantee that herein lies the start of your rehabilitation. I recommend keeping this document to yourself for at least ten years. You can then take it out to read it and remind yourself of your past dreams, like I did recently. I suspect that you will have a very spooky experience when you do.

Firstly, I live exactly the life today that I wrote about ten years ago – I have achieved my dreams. I have attended the Super Bowl, the men's Wimbledon tennis final and the rugby World Cup final. I have attended events and been on trips that I hadn't even imagined. I have been on multiple safaris and a variety of Caribbean cruises, as well as other cruises all over the world, many of which I have been paid to go on! I am a certified scuba diver, I can play the guitar (poorly), I live in the sun all year round, I have a beautiful family, and my businesses have produced tens of millions of dollars. I have spoken to up to 5,000 people at one time.

Not one of these dreams was real to me when I wrote them down that very first time. The difference between a dream and a goal is that one doesn't have a plan and the other does. Get writing, make it real and suddenly you will become very protective of your time! If you run out of paper during the exercise and require more space to write, use the notes section at the start of the planner.

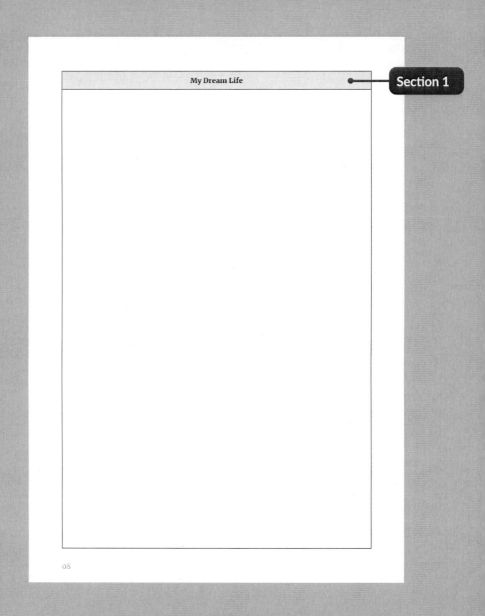

My Dream Life — Section 1

Figure 3.1 RETHINK! Planner – My Dream Life (Section 1)

More information on this is in Psalm 12.3.1 in *Rethink Time Management.*

The next stage after writing out your hopes and dreams is to coalesce these dreams and start to move them out of the ideas realm (for now) by putting some realistic timelines around them and turning them into goals.

The first thing that I'd like you to do is take what you have written down in your wish list and to start to organise the items into specific, one-sentence goals. If you have written something like "I'm in the Bahamas, and I'm having a fantastic time" as a description of your dream life, you can modify this to "I am visiting the Bahamas by the 15th of March 2030, and I'm spending two weeks there on a cruise."

The writing of goals in a specific format is critical. There are lots of theories around this, but the tried and tested SMART format for documenting goals still has its place here. I prefer to use a more advanced version of this called SMARTER goals.

Firstly, goals must be expressed in the present tense, using the language of "I am" rather than "I will be". Then you can start following the guidance within the SMARTER acronym to lead you through the rest of the process. As you can see below, the letters may stand for a variety of different words, but all generally mean the same thing. Specific (simple, sensible, significant) Measurable (meaningful, motivating) Achievable (agreed, attainable) Relevant (realistic, resourced, results-based) Time-bound (time-based, time-limited, time or cost limited, timely, time-sensitive) Evaluated (expectations, enriched values, estimated) Reviewed (reasonable, researched).

Once you have written the "What" and the "When", then make an assessment into which of the 8 *RETHINK!* areas is most suitable as a label for each goal in turn.

My Dreams to Reality		
What	When	RETHiNK! Area

Section 2

09

Figure 3.2 RETHINK! Planner – My Dreams to Reality (Section 2)

More information on this is in Psalm 12.3.2 in Rethink Time Management.

The next part relates to your vision for the future you in each *RETHINK!* area. Once you have organised your goals by area, you can then look at the goals you have in each area and start to group them.

Whatever you have for "Health" (for example), group all of those goals together. Whatever you have for "Earnings", group them together, and so on. This will allow you to create a vision of your future self that you'd like to see in each area of your life. You now have written goals for each area, and you'll probably start to see a picture or a clear theme or direction indicating what you truly want from life, as opposed to the all-too-common feeling of being a little lost.

Once you have grouped your goals this way, you can start to look at the goals you have in each area, in order to identify trends and see what the common themes are in relation to your goals. When you have completed this for all areas, I'd advise you to draw up a four or five-sentence vision statement that outlines where you see yourself being in each area of your life. I haven't given a whole lot of room for this in the workbook, because it is just an overall vision of where you see yourself being in each Rethink! Area.

My Vision	Section 3
Relationships	
Earnings	
Tao	
Health	
Investments	
Networks	
Knowledge	
! Fun	

10

Figure 3.3 RETHINK! Planner – My Vision (Section 3)

More information on this is in Psalm 12.3.3 in *Rethink Time Management*.

Having got some clarity on what you would love to do, be and have over the next few years, you can now start to build a structure around your medium to longer-term goals, and feed them into the *RETHINK! Planner*. The next step is to complete your 10-15-year goal template.

"Why 15 years?" you may ask. Well, it started as a 10-year plan, and having had the experience of looking at the results and expectations of thousands of clients, I have noticed that people, including me, tend to be quite optimistic about what they can do in 10 years. Interestingly, I have found that most people find it very difficult to think beyond or project beyond a 10-year timeline. Even 10 years is a real push for them.

That doesn't mean you won't have 15-year goals. As a general rule of thumb, you can add an extra 50% in years to your initial plan in order to get a more realistic figure for how long it will take to achieve. This is how you arrive at your 15-year plan.

When we think in terms of day-to-day timelines, we restrict our creative abilities. We constrain ourselves to small-minded thinking within short timespans. J.K. Rowling had a clear plan that she was going to write seven books in the Harry Potter series before she even sat down to start the first. Putting longer-term perspectives in place is crucial, because if we don't think over extended periods of time, we can't think big, and this limits our present and future opportunities. Don't be afraid to think BIG. What is the worst that can happen?

I would like you to take your goals from Figure 3.2 – My Dreams to Reality and organise and set out your overall goals in each area of your life for the next 15 years. This is going to take a little time. It's great that you have already sat down and gone through your goals in each area, but they are most likely very mixed in terms of the natural timelines you have set for yourself. Now it is time to take a longer-term view. You will start with 15-year goals, and from there you will work backwards to arrive at daily actions.

You will find this quite a powerful exercise – most of us rarely think further ahead than a one or two-year timeframe, but here you have the opportunity to think 15 years into the future. In my case, I thought, "Oh yeah, sure I'll eventually leave my job and eventually do something that I want to do," but without a plan, it remained a dream. As soon as I started to write it down as a goal and was forced to think it through, the realisation suddenly dawned on me that unless I had a specific plan for how I was going to achieve my goal, it was never going to happen. Why? Because, quite simply, there is always a reason that now is not the right time.

Section 4

Goals	6 Months	1 Year	2-3 Years
Relationships			
Earnings			
Tao			
Health			
Investments			
Networks			
Knowledge			
! Fun			

My 15 Year Goals

12

Figure 3.4 RETHINK! Planner – My 15-Year Goals (Section 4)

In the first column you will see the different eight Rethink! areas for which you are setting your goals. To speed up the process, start with the areas that come more naturally to you – this will help you get into an inspired flow. Each of the columns on the right-hand side has timelines from six months up to 10-15 years.

You may notice that from year two onwards I have grouped timelines spanning a few years: 2-3 years, 4-6 years, 7-10 years and 10-15 years. The reason for this is that it is challenging to be very specific for each year if you have never done this exercise before. You may be unaware of your future capabilities and may find it difficult to predict specifically when you will be able to complete certain goals. This method allows you to become more specific over time as you move towards your goals.

I recommend you start on the far right-hand side and think about where you want to be in 15 years' time. In this table, there is only room for one main goal for each life area. That is more than enough for now, believe me! Take your time on this. This process is not meant to be rushed; it is a tool to unlock your inner genius, allowing you to set and achieve big, bold targets.

This forward-looking process allows you to start at the furthest point in the future and work backwards from there. You will think, "Okay, if that's where I want to be in 10-15 years, where do I need to be in 7-10 years? Where do I need to be in five years, three years, next year or in six months' time? What's my first step today?"

If you have more than one goal per area after completing your dream life exercise, prioritise the top goal for each area. Make your 15-year targets for the goals you have chosen in each area both motivational and inspirational for you. There's no point in having a target that isn't going to drive you forwards. If it doesn't inspire you then it is not truly a goal worthy of this list. The whole point of having a goal in 15 years' time is that it makes you think, "I'm really motivated to do this, I'm really inspired to do this, and I'm going to do what I need to do to achieve this."

More information on this is in Psalm 13.1 in *Rethink Time Management*.

Your next step is to look at each of the eight areas in Figure 3.4 and ensure that the overriding goal that you wish to achieve over a 10-to-15-year timeframe in each area is the BIG one you choose to go after. (There is an exercise to help with this in Psalm 13.2 of *Rethink Time Management*). Some of the goals for specific areas will take a lot more focus than others, and that is precisely how it should be. In areas on which you don't place much value, you can set much easier-to-achieve targets, but you will not be ignoring that aspect of your life, which is the important thing. Most people will end up valuing each one of the areas most highly at one point in their lives.

Let's look at an example. Imagine your earning goal is to be financially free in 15 years. You can work backwards in your 7-10 year, 4-6 year, 2-3 year goals and so on, adding in the specific milestones needed to reach the end goal. Achieving that one big goal 15 years from now will require a series of goals that cascade down, which you can factor into your shorter-term planning a little later. Now, before getting into any more detail, you want to make sure these big eight are truly the goals you want to go after.

My Annual Goals

Annual RETHiNK! Goals		
Relationships		by
Earnings		by
Tao		by
Health		by
Investments		by
Networks		by
Knowledge		by
! Fun		by

Figure 3.5 RETHINK! Planner – Yearly RETHINK! Goals (Section 5)

3.1 Turning Your Annual Goals into Weekly Targets

The planner begins with Figures 3.6 and 3.7, which allow you to identify your targets.

Warren Buffet famously said, *"If you can't read the scoreboard, you don't know the score. If you don't know the score, you can't tell the winners from the losers."* Simply put, if you don't know where you are going, it's difficult to know when you arrive!

Without this starting point, none of the rest of the planner has any real meaning. I will break these down by section to make it super easy for you to follow along.

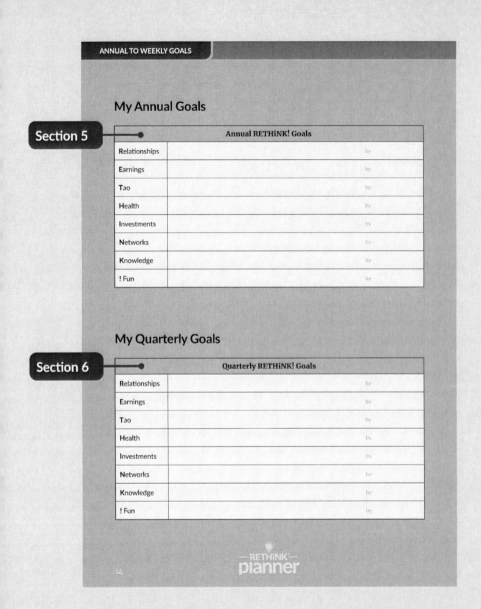

ANNUAL TO WEEKLY GOALS

My Annual Goals

Section 5

Annual RETHiNK! Goals		
Relationships		by
Earnings		by
Tao		by
Health		by
Investments		by
Networks		by
Knowledge		by
! Fun		by

My Quarterly Goals

Section 6

Quarterly RETHiNK! Goals		
Relationships		by
Earnings		by
Tao		by
Health		by
Investments		by
Networks		by
Knowledge		by
! Fun		by

RETHiNK
planner

14

Figure 3.6 RETHINK! Planner – Yearly and Quarterly Planner Pages (Section 5 and 6)

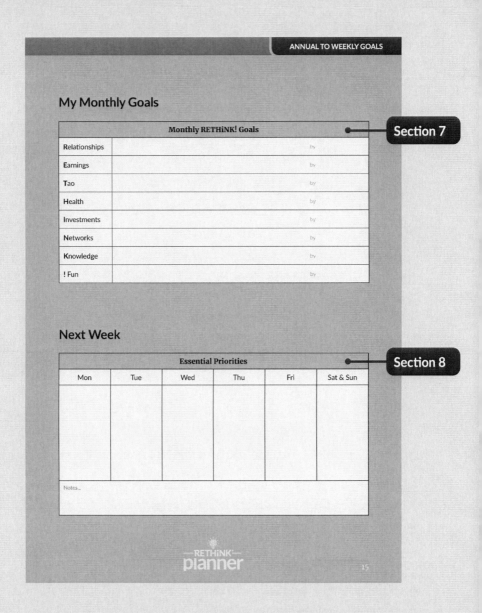

My Monthly Goals

Monthly RETHiNK! Goals		
Relationships		by
Earnings		by
Tao		by
Health		by
Investments		by
Networks		by
Knowledge		by
! Fun		by

Section 7

Next Week

Essential Priorities					
Mon	Tue	Wed	Thu	Fri	Sat & Sun

Notes...

Section 8

RETHiNK planner

15

Figure 3.7 RETHINK! Planner – Monthly and Weekly Planner Pages (Sections 7 and 8)

Now let's break these sections down for you in turn. Turn to the very start of your planner, and let's begin with your foundation step in Section 5.

Section 5:

In this section, you start by completing your goals for each of these eight areas by the *end of the current year.*

My Annual Goals

	Annual RETHiNK! Goals	
Relationships		by
Earnings		by
Tao		by
Health	I am exercising daily for a minimum of 15 minutes and have a resting heart rate of 55 bpm and body fat of 15% or less	by 31 Dec 2030
Investments		by
Networks		by
Knowledge		by
! Fun		by

Figure 3.8 RETHINK! Planner – Yearly RETHINK! Goals (Section 5)

In the last chapter – 2.0 What is *"RETHiNK!"*? – I requested that you write out goals for the end of the year in SMARTER format, and I provided this example:

"I am exercising daily for a minimum of 15 minutes and have a resting heart rate of 55 bpm and body fat of 15% or less by 31st of December 2030 or sooner."

The "by" word within the template on each line is the division point between the goal itself and the date to have achieved it "by". Now go ahead and fill out these "Year End" details for the end of your current year right at the start of the planner, in part 4.

In Figure 3.8, I have an example of exactly how to do this for your end of year "health" goal. Once this task is complete, you are ready for Section 6.

Section 6:

Your next task is to identify where you need to be by the end of *your current quarter* to hit this end of year goal. You will do this every quarter to identify the end of current quarter goals. Assuming you are starting in quarter one of the year, all dates will be "by" end of quarter one (Q1) of the year which is 31 March. In quarter two (Q2) all dates will be "by 30 June". Q3 ends on 30 September and Q4 on 31 December.

My Quarterly Goals

Quarterly RETHiNK! Goals		
Relationships		by
Earnings		by
Tao		by
Health	*I am exercising daily for a minimum of 8 minutes and have a resting heart rate of 65 bpm and body fat of 22% or less*	by *31 Mar 2030*
Investments		by
Networks		by
Knowledge		by
! Fun		by

Figure 3.9 RETHINK! Planner – Next Quarter RETHINK! Goals (Section 6)

Taking the annual goal example from earlier, "I am exercising daily for a minimum of 15 minutes and have a resting heart rate of 55 bpm and body fat of 15% or less by 31st of December 2030 or sooner", you now need to set a reasonable goal for quarter one (Q1) of the year.

Let's assume that the end of Q1 goal would become: "I am exercising daily for a minimum of **8 minutes** and have a resting heart rate of **65 bpm** and body fat of **22%** or less by **31st of March 2030** or sooner". See how this has been added to Figure 3.9.

Now you can set your own Q1 targets on the way to your year-end goals. Fill out the details for the end of your current quarter for each of the eight areas in turn, identifying your end-of-quarter target.

Section 7:

You are probably getting the hang of this by now. Your next step is to take the quarterly goals and break them down into monthly chunks, starting with the current month of the quarter you are in. It may be the first, second or third month of the quarter, depending on when you start using this planner.

My Monthly Goals

	Monthly RETHiNK! Goals	
Relationships		by
Earnings		by
Tao		by
Health	I am exercising daily for a minimum of 6 minutes and have a resting heart rate of 70 bpm and body fat of 25% or less	by 31 Jan 2030
Investments		by
Networks		by
Knowledge		by
! Fun		by

Figure 3.10 RETHINK! Planner – Next Month RETHINK! Goals (Section 7)

Taking the example Q1 goal, which was "I am exercising daily for a minimum of **8 minutes** and have a resting heart rate of **65 bpm** and body fat of **22%** or less by **31st of March 2030** or sooner", you can now turn this into a monthly goal for month one of the quarter.

This could look something like: "I am exercising daily for a minimum of **6 minutes** and have a resting heart rate of **70 bpm** and body fat of **25%** or less by **31st of January 2030** or sooner". This has been added to Figure 3.10.

At this point, your seemingly insurmountable annual goal is now chunked down from a quarterly target to an end-of-month target, which leaves just one more set of targets: your weekly target.

Feel free once more to fill out these details for your goals for the end of your current month in part 4 of the planner.

Section 8:

You are definitely getting the hang of this! You now have the relatively easy task of taking a month-end goal and placing some key targets into your weekly "Essential Priorities" to ensure you keep on track. This enables you to plan in more "real time", as you are only a week away from targets, and to be aware of any time blockages that could interfere.

Next Week

| | Essential Priorities | | | | |
Mon	Tue	Wed	Thu	Fri	Sat & Sun
			Hospital Apt – 10am – 2pm		

Notes...

Figure 3.11 RETHINK! Planner – Next Week Essential Priorities (Section 8)

Even at the weekly stage of planning, you continue to keep your monthly targets as your main focus. Use this weekly planner to identify what you can do this week to get you closer to achieving those end-of-month goals.

Use each day to map out clear outcomes you would ideally like to achieve to keep you on track to achieving your goals by the end of the month.

Now, one last time, you can fill out these details for the upcoming week. You're ready to rock and roll!

3.2 Using Your Daily Planner

It's time to take a look at what a "daily" page looks like in its entirety before breaking it down section by section. I use sun and moon symbols to indicate whether you fill out each section in the morning or the evening.

In total, the page should take no longer than ten minutes to complete in its entirety. If you can't make ten minutes to plan and track your day, you are probably working on someone else's goals. Imagine just ten minutes a day to a brand new life!

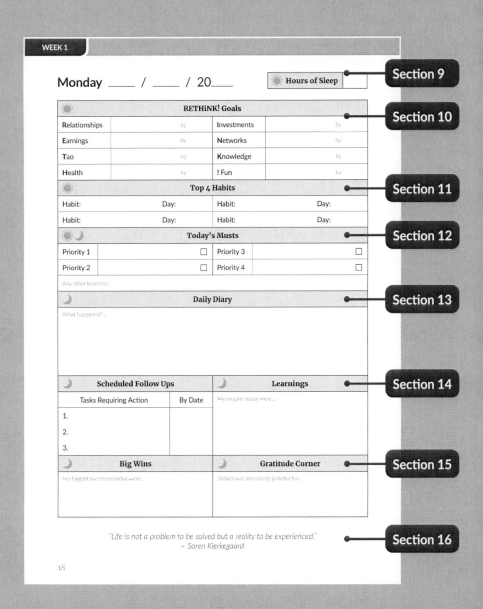

WEEK 1

Monday ___ / ___ / 20___

Hours of Sleep — **Section 9**

RETHiNK! Goals — **Section 10**

Relationships	by	Investments	by
Earnings	by	Networks	by
Tao	by	Knowledge	by
Health	by	! Fun	by

Top 4 Habits — **Section 11**

Habit:	Day:	Habit:	Day:
Habit:	Day:	Habit:	Day:

Today's Musts — **Section 12**

Priority 1	☐	Priority 3	☐
Priority 2	☐	Priority 4	☐

Any other business...

Daily Diary — **Section 13**

What happened?...

Scheduled Follow Ups / Learnings — **Section 14**

Tasks Requiring Action	By Date	My insights today were...
1.		
2.		
3.		

Big Wins / Gratitude Corner — **Section 15**

My biggest successes today were... | Today I was immensely grateful for...

"Life is not a problem to be solved but a reality to be experienced." — **Section 16**
– Soren Kierkegaard

18

Figure 3.12 RETHINK! Planner – Daily Page

Section 9:

You start at the top with Section 9, which already includes the week number within that quarter of the year and the day of the week.

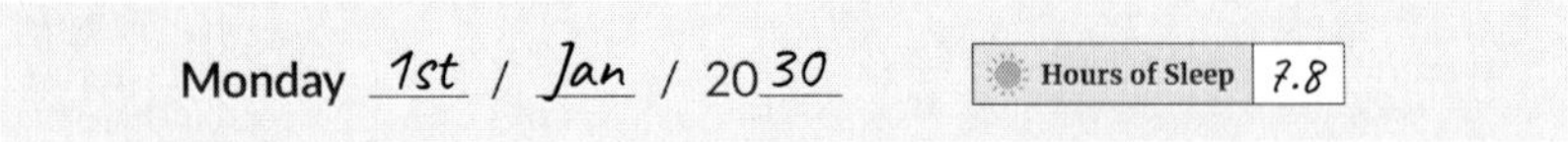

Monday _1st_ / _Jan_ / 20 _30_   ☀ **Hours of Sleep** | _7.8_

Figure 3.13 RETHINK! Planner – Daily Page (Section 9)

Each day, write out the date in the format you are familiar with – US or European style. You can start to use the planner at any time of the year. For ease of use, I recommend you go directly to the week number of the quarter you are in on your first day using the planner. If you start from there, it will line up nicely with month-end and quarter-end pages in the planner.

For example, if you pick this planner up on Tuesday 22nd of January, I recommend skipping to the Tuesday of Week 4 of the planner (although this is not absolutely necessary). I include 15 weeks in every quarter, which gives you an allowance of 5 weeks per month. This makes it easier for you to choose which week of the quarter you are in whenever you start using the planner.

On the right-hand side, you should fill out how many hours you slept the night before. I use a Whoop watch to track this every night, and it gives a readout on my phone in the morning. You can get the Whoop strap FREE and your first month FREE when you join using this link **bit.ly/whooppaul**

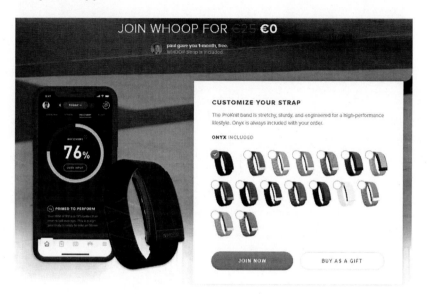

Alternatives include an aura ring, a Fitbit, an Apple Watch or a smartphone app like Sleep Cycle, which will all track your sleep. At a bare minimum, if you can't track your sleep this way, you can make a note of it based on the time you went to bed and the time you woke up (although we know this usually isn't the same as actual hours of sleep, but it's a step in the right direction). The number of hours you sleep has a direct correlation with how productive you are daily, and this is too often overlooked.

NB: You should also notice the sun icon ☀ beside "Hours of Sleep". This is used as a guide as to what time of the day you should fill out the information. In this case, you fill out Section 9 in the morning, as the sun rises (although not necessarily at the crack of dawn!). This should take no longer than 30 seconds to complete.

Section 10:

In this section, you will take the goals you have identified in your quarterly targets in Section 6 and add them here for each of the eight areas.

☀	RETHiNK! Goals			
Relationships	by	Investments		by
Earnings	by	Networks		by
Tao	by	Knowledge		by
Health	>8m<65bpm<22%b by 31/3/30	! Fun		by

Figure 3.14 RETHINK! Planner – Daily Page (Section 10)

In Sections 5-8, you have already identified your yearly, quarterly, month and week-end goals. In this section, you fill out what your end-of-quarter goals are. You will also note that there are blanks to be filled in around the word "by". This is to encourage you daily to get into the habit of quickly writing down the goal that you are going to achieve, and by when.

I suggest you put your end-of-quarter goal into your daily log, since anything further into the future is too far away, and anything nearer-term may appear to arrive too quickly. Quarterly goals have worked best for me after years of trial and error. Start each day by writing in your quarterly goal in each of the life areas, and remember that you have a spare buffer week at the end of each quarter when you measure your time in weeks as opposed to months!

Assuming you are starting in quarter one of the year, all dates will be "by" end of quarter one of the year, which is 31st of March 20XX.

As before, let's assume that the end-of-quarter Q1 goal would be: "I am exercising daily for a minimum of **8 minutes** and have a resting heart rate of **65 bpm** and body fat of 22% or less by **31st of March 2030** or sooner".

As the space is confined in the daily planner pages (and to save time), you now write the goal in shorthand form. This health goal would now become something like ">8m <65bpm <22%bf" which summarises all the key measurables in shorthand form (greater than 8 minutes, less than 65 beats per minute and less than 22% body fat).

You can see this demonstrated in Figure 3.14. Each day, once you have completed Section 9, you will hand write the short form of your goals for each of the eight areas, so you start every day knowing what your overall goals are. This is therefore an incredibly powerful tool for reminding you what personal goals you are working towards in each area. This makes it much easier for you to decide what to prioritise and what to say a polite "no" to during your day.

Note: This section includes the sun icon ☀ which means it is filled in during the morning. This goals section, when using shorthand, should take no longer than 90 seconds to complete each day, as you are writing down the same quarterly goals each day of the quarter.

Section 11:

In Section 11, "Top 4 Habits", I invite you to put together a list of habits that you will need to add to your daily routine (like a daily jog) or remove from your daily routine (like drinking alcohol) to build the behaviours that will allow you to hit your goals on autopilot. You will then pick only two from this list of habits.

☀	Top 4 Habits			
Habit: *Fill out Daily Planner*	Day: 22	Habit:	Day:
Habit:	Day:	Habit:	Day:

Figure 3.15 RETHINK! Planner – Daily Page (Section 11)

In Psalm 7.0 of *Rethink Time Management*, I dive into the detail behind the formation of habits and how this tool allows you to easily hit the minimum requirement of 66 consecutive days to form a new habit.

This is exactly how I managed to achieve and track all the habits I mentioned a little earlier, and which are listed again here. I started with a single habit and built from there. The key is choosing small achievable habits, that you can do consistently without much motivation and adding no more than two at a time and tracking progress with your planner.

- Jog every day for 1,492 days in a row

- Cut sugar out of my diet for 1,050 days (excluding fruit, vegetables and alcohol!)

- Eat no bread for 704 days

- Eat no cheese for 704 days

- Include greens in my diet for 623 days

- Include probiotics in my diet for 623 days

- Do "energy clearing" daily for 520 days (more information available on page 153 of the *RETHINK! Planner* section)

- Lift weights daily for 230 days

- Drink Alkaline Iodised Water daily for 180 days (more information available on page 152 of the *RETHINK! Planner* section)

- Have a cold shower for 95 days

Over time, once certain habits were embedded, I moved to the next four to track those. Without getting too deep into this, as it is covered in the book Rethink Time Management, my recommendations are as follows.

As I said, it is best to choose no more than two new habits a quarter, regardless of how eager you are ☺. I strongly recommend starting with your very first new habit being the act of filling out your daily planner. The second habit could be to take a brisk walk or jog every single day while listening to an audiobook. Each day you write into the log what the habit is and how many days you have done it for, as shown in Figure 3.10. These habits will stack and build upon each other over time, and you will get to experience compounded benefits.

Here's the crucial part: If you miss a day, any day, **your day count resets to zero** and you must start again! The goal is to get to at least a full quarter, which is 90 days, carrying out that habit until it is locked in. Then you can add two more habits the next quarter. This will change your life beyond recognition, as it did for me – and tens of thousands of my clients!

You will notice that there is space for four different habits that can be tracked at any one time. Once you have a quarter's habits embedded, you no longer need to track them, and you can add your next two to the tracking list as Habits 3 and 4.

Note: This section includes the sun icon ☀ which means it is filled in during the morning. It will take you less than 30 seconds to fill in.

Section 12:

Now you can move on to the next section, which is "Today's Musts". This is where you identify the biggest four tasks of the day towards achieving your goals. Sometimes this is referred to as the tasks that "move the needle" the most in the direction of measurable progress for you.

☀ ☽	Today's Musts		
Priority 1	*Meet personal trainer* ☒	Priority 3	☐
Priority 2	☐	Priority 4	☐
Any other business...			

Figure 3.16 RETHINK! Planner – Daily Page (Section 12)

You need to ensure that you always have a slightly bigger picture in mind before getting started on your daily priorities. This is why you start the day by first reminding yourself of the goals in each area for the end of the quarter. There is room for "Any other business" where you can add other tasks to get through when your top four priorities are completed. Some days a priority might be as simple as getting to a dentist's appointment; they do not need to be earth-shattering!

There is a tick box to acknowledge at the end of the day if each task was completed. If not, it may need to be carried forward.

Note: This section includes the sun icon ☀ which means the priorities are filled in during the morning in less than one minute. It also has the moon icon ☽ to show that you fill out the tick boxes at the end of the day in about 30 seconds.

Section 13:

This next section is the "Daily Diary" itself, which is what I use to track what I do on a daily basis, very much like a traditional diary.

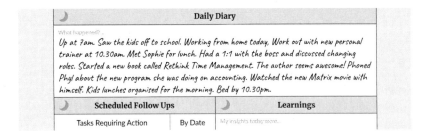

Figure 3.17 RETHINK! Planner – Daily Page (Section 13)

As you can see, there is not a whole lot of space. This is intentional, as you only touch upon the key highlights of the day. It should be just enough that when you look back at it in a year, you can remember the day.

Note: This section includes the moon icon ☽ to acknowledge that you fill out a quick summary of your primary tasks at the end of the day in two minutes maximum. It should not be a history lesson ☺

Section 14:

Immediately underneath the "Daily Diary" are two elements, "Scheduled Follow Ups" and "Learnings".

Scheduled Follow Ups		Learnings
Tasks Requiring Action	By Date	My insights today were...
1. New eating plan	24 Jan '30	I ate at 8.30pm last night and my sleep quality percentage dropped by 15%
2.		
3.		

Figure 3.18 RETHINK! Planner – Daily Page (Section 14)

"Scheduled Follow Ups" is where you take the pre-planned priorities that did not get done on that day as you had hoped, or new items that have come up and now need to be planned into your future agenda. The key element with each of these is to clearly identify the due date by which they need to be done so that you can organise the tasks later in terms of urgency.

The "Learnings" section is adopted from the US Marine Corps, who use something similar to track what they learned about themselves each day. I insist that I do this every single day, to ensure that every day is a school day and the subject is "me" – I am constantly looking for new insights about myself. If you wish, you can identify specific areas that worked well during the day and those that did not.

Note: This section includes the moon icon ☽ to show that you fill out a quick summary of your follow-up tasks and your learnings at the end of the day in one minute or less each.

Section 15:

In Section 15, I quickly identify what I am thankful for in the "Big Wins", no matter how big or small. However poorly the day appears to go, I always insist on identifying at least a couple of things that went well, and this could be as small as "I used my daily planner". This is a very powerful habit, as it forces you to be positively focused at the end of each day. On the right-hand side, you will find "Gratitude Corner".

Big Wins	Gratitude Corner
My biggest successes today were ..	Today I was immensely grateful for..
Jess won her singing competition	Phyl took time to go over how I can easily manage my home budget with this new tool that she is using

Figure 3.19 RETHINK! Planner – Daily Page (Section 15)

The act of gratitude has long been recognised as one of the most powerful forces a person can harness to fast-track progress in their life. Some people write entire gratitude logs each day! For this planner, at the end of the day, I quickly identify what I am thankful, for no matter how big or small, in one or more of the eight areas of life.

Note: This section includes the moon icon ☽ to show that you fill out a quick summary of your wins and what you are grateful for at the end of the day in one minute or less each.

Section 16:

In the last section, I reference one quotation or mantra each day.

"Life is not a problem to be solved but a reality to be experienced."
– Soren Kierkegaard

Figure 3.20 RETHINK! Planner – Daily Page (Section 16)

The quote I include in this section every day may be from one of my own books, one of the books I have read or from a catalogue of quotes that I have kept over the years. I find it very inspiring to read just one simple quote a day. I hope that the quotes you see daily land at exactly the right time for you to hear them!

3.3 Weekly Summary

You are now ready to look at what a weekly summary page looks like. We'll break it down into its two elements: reflecting and planning the week ahead.

The good news is that you have done most of the work already by filling out your daily pages. Reflection on the week gone by is just as important as planning for the week ahead so that you learn from your "mistakes" and spot trends. A typical trend is to be over-ambitious with setting your weekly targets. When you review this weekly, you can very quickly adjust accordingly for the next week, either by pulling back on the aggressiveness of your goals or by bringing resources on board to support you in achieving the tasks on schedule. The *RETHINK! Planner* is set up to ensure that you can both reflect and plan.

WEEK 1

Weekly Review

RETHiNK! Reflections	
Relationships	
Earnings	
Tao	
Health	
Investments	
Networks	
Knowledge	
! Fun	

Notes...

Section 17

Next Week

Essential Priorities					
Mon	Tue	Wed	Thu	Fri	Sat & Sun

Notes...

Section 8

RETHiNK
planner

25

Section 17:

In the "Weekly Review" section, you are invited to reflect on each of the eight areas.

Weekly Review

RETHiNK! Reflections	
Relationships	*I did not prioritised my partner even one day this week again!*
Earnings	
Tao	
Health	
Investments	
Networks	
Knowledge	
! Fun	
Notes...	

Figure 3.21 RETHINK! Planner – Weekly Review (Section 17)

As you do this, just fill in a simple one-liner learning what you have noticed. Perhaps you have been overly ambitious in one area, and in another area, you have hit your target with ease and could become slightly more aggressive with your targets.

When you do this weekly, every single week you will become much better at planning for the week ahead with more accuracy. In time you'll become a complete pro!

The "Next Week" section is identical to Section 4, where you are invited at the start of each new week to identify on a daily calendar the key highlights of the week to come.

Next Week

	Essential Priorities				
Mon	Tue	Wed	Thu	Fri	Sat & Sun
			Hospital Apt – 10am – 2pm		

Notes...

Figure 3.22 RETHINK! Planner – Next Week Essential Priorities (Section 4; shown in Figure 3.7)

This allows you to identify any major time blocks that could take away from your overall intentions towards achieving your goals so that you can adjust accordingly.

Use each day to map out clear outcomes you would ideally like to achieve to keep you on track to achieving your bigger goals by the end of the month.

3.4 Monthly Summary

Much like the weekly summary, you then review how the month performed as a whole.

You will note the term "optional" at the top of the page. This is here because you may feel that weekly check-ins are enough for you. Personally, I prefer to do the weekly and monthly reviews, as the monthly review also serves as a scorecard on monthly performance and a collated review of all weekly learnings.

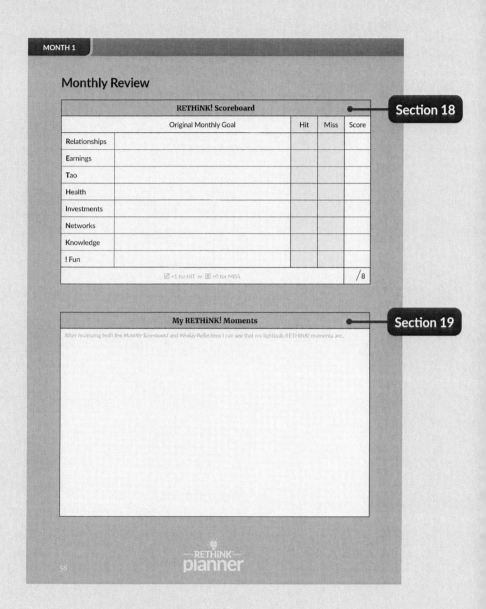

Figure 3.23 RETHINK! Planner – Monthly RETHINK! Scoreboard and Moments (Sections 18 and 19)

Section 18:

In Section 18, the *"RETHINK! Scoreboard"*, you can do a very simple yet powerful check on your monthly performance, which is scored out of 8 based on how many of your monthly targets you hit across your 8 areas of life. The maximum score you can get is a perfect 8/8. For simplicity, 1 for a hit or 0 for a miss is best. It's up to you if you choose to give yourself fractional scores, like 0.5, if you feel you made it a fraction of the way to your goal.

Monthly Review

RETHiNK! Scoreboard				
	Original Monthly Goal	Hit	Miss	Score
Relationships				
Earnings				
Tao				
Health	*I am exercising daily for a minimum of 6 minutes and have a resting heart rate of 70 bpm and body fat of 25% or less*	✓		*1*
Investments				
Networks				
Knowledge				
! Fun				
	☑ +1 for HIT or ☒ +0 for MISS			/8

Figure 3.24 RETHINK! Planner – Monthly Review RETHINK! Scoreboard (Section 18)

Section 19:

Much like the weekly summary, there is a reflections element – "My *RETHINK!* Moments" – which is a summary of the weekly reflections for that month.

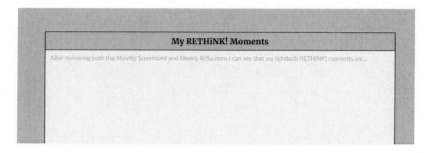

Figure 3.25 RETHINK! Planner – Monthly Review RETHINK! Moments (Section 19)

After this section, you are now ready for the all-important "CLEAR OUT!" The intention here is to get rid of as many items as possible from your "Follow Up" lists.

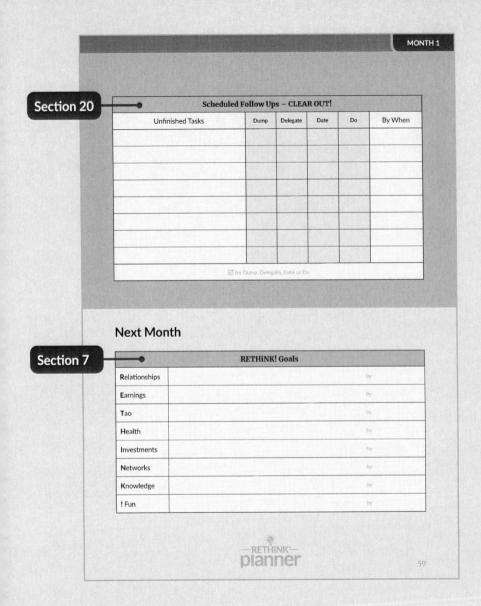

Figure 3.26 RETHINK! Planner – Monthly Clear Out and Goals (Sections 20 and 7)

Section 20:

In this section, "Scheduled Follow Ups – CLEAR OUT!", you will perform your monthly spring clean. You will go back over all open follow-up items that have been carried through each week and list them all in the "Unfinished Tasks" column.

You will then look at each task in turn and perform a "4D" assessment. This is where you choose a course of action for each task: completely "dump" as your first option, "delegate" to someone else as the next best option, set a "date" for future completion as your third option, if you need to do it but not necessarily today, and, finally, "do" for tasks that need to get done within the next 24 hours. This allows you to clearly prioritise your tasks as you head into a new week.

Tick the appropriate box depending on which action can be taken with each unfinished task.

Scheduled Follow Ups – CLEAR OUT!					
Unfinished Tasks	Dump	Delegate	Date	Do	By When
Book meeting with accountant			✓		
Perform review of old emails		Mary			
Wisdom tooth appointment				✓	
New backup pc for the office	✓				
☑ for Dump, Delegate, Date or Do					

Figure 3.27 RETHINK! Planner – Monthly Clear Out (Section 20)

3.5 Quarterly Summary

Finally, at the end of each quarter, you will do a check-in on performance once more.

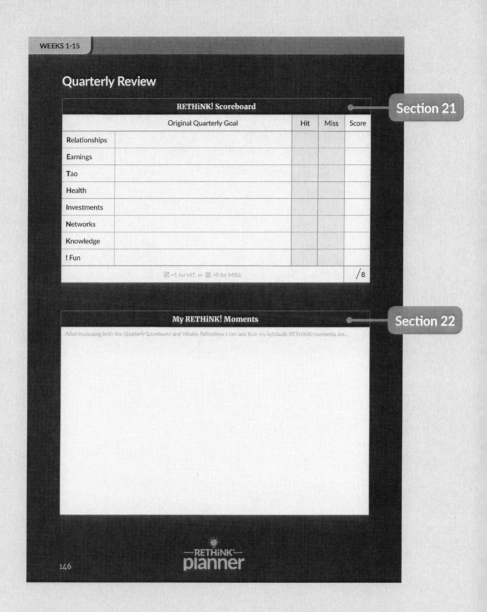

Figure 3.28 RETHINK! Planner – Quarterly Review and Moments (Sections 21 and 22)

Section 21:

In Section 21, you complete a score-based review of the quarter, exactly as you did for the end-of-month review. The maximum score is 8/8 for the quarter, or 32/32 for an entire year. That would be pretty epic!

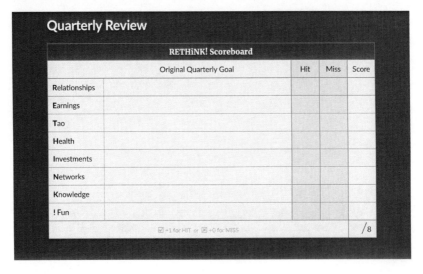

Quarterly Review				
RETHiNK! Scoreboard				
	Original Quarterly Goal	Hit	Miss	Score
Relationships				
Earnings				
Tao				
Health				
Investments				
Networks				
Knowledge				
! Fun				
☑ +1 for HIT or ☒ +0 for MISS				/8

Figure 3.29 RETHINK! Planner – Quarterly Review RETHINK! Scoreboard (Section 21)

Section 22:

In Section 22, you collate the main learnings from the previous three months into the quarterly review.

Figure 3.30 RETHINK! Planner – Quarterly Review RETHINK! Moments (Section 22)

Just as before, you are asked to do a spring clean of tasks that have built up over the quarter in Section 23.

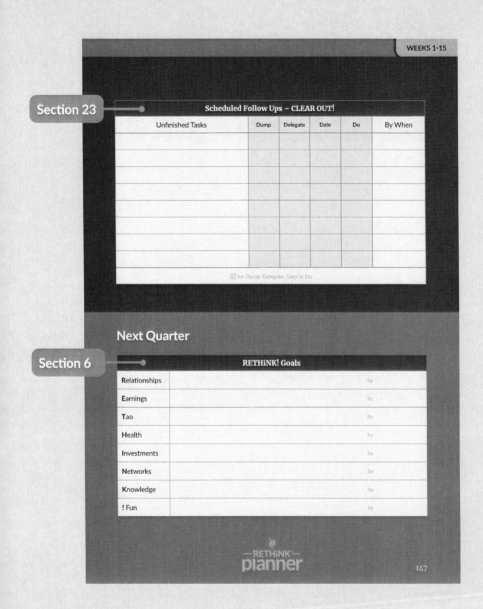

Figure 3.31 RETHINK! Planner – Quarterly Clear Out and RETHINK! Goals (Sections 23 and 6)

Section 23:

In this section, "Scheduled Follow Ups – CLEAR OUT!", you are going to perform the same task described in Section 16 for the month, but this time for the quarter. You will go back over all open follow-up items that have been carried through each month, list them in the "Unfinished Tasks" column and carry out the "4D" assessment.

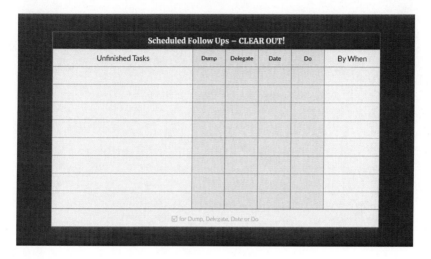

Scheduled Follow Ups – CLEAR OUT!					
Unfinished Tasks	Dump	Delegate	Date	Do	By When

☑ for Dump, Delegate, Date or Do

Figure 3.32 RETHINK! Planner – Quarterly Clear Out (Section 23)

As a final step, you will identify what your goals are for the upcoming quarter using the upcoming quarterly goals that you used in Section 6. This time, it is for the next quarter.

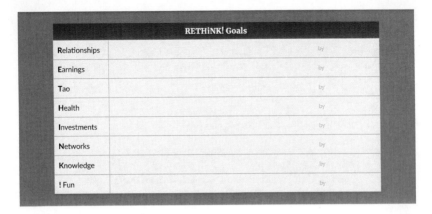

Figure 3.33 RETHINK! Planner – Next Quarter RETHINK! Goals (Section 6, as shown in Figure 3.6)

You are now 100% graduated and ready to utilise the next part of your *RETHINK! Planner*

I wish you all the very best with your use of this and am very excited for the results this will help you achieve. Please ensure that you order your next quarter's planner in plenty of time so that you keep that momentum going.

We have created a series of videos to supplement your training, which are available at **www.rethinkplanner.com/startguide**

RETHiNK
TIME MANAGEMENT

...G.O.D.'S Guide to Heaven on Earth is transforming lives! Jim Rohn is quoted as saying
"Time is more valuable than money, you can make more money, but you can't make more time!"

While that's technically true, Rethink Time Management
is going to show you how you can make more time.

Learn more at: **www.RethinkTimeManagement.com**

RETHiNK
TIME MANAGEMENT
COURSE

...gives you additional training, insights, and time hacks, on how to use the Rethink Planner and the various frameworks contained in the Rethink Time Management book.

The course also goes into a proven monthly review and priority process and project planning process that will help you improve your focus, stay on track, overcome overwhelm, boost your productivity and outsource your busy work.

Learn more at:
www.RethinkTimeManagement.com/course

Other books in the RETHiNK Series

**RETHiNK
SOCIAL MEDIA**
Instead of using social media purely for entertainment, why not use it to make money?

**RETHiNK
SOCIAL MEDIA
ADVERTISING**
Utilise the full power of Facebook advertising to help your business.

**RETHiNK
MONEY FOR TEENS
AND CHILDREN**
Provides the tools needed to create more, save more, and grow more money.

Alkaline Ionised Water

Something that has made a huge difference in my daily and weekly routine is the many benefits from investing in an Alkaline Ionised water unit.

There are different units out there on the market for sale and personal, I want the BEST for me and my family. If this is something you are interested in I would encourage you to check out the man I dealt with as he was very helpful and supportive.

Here is his website to dive deeper into learning more about this water technology: **www.RethinkPlanner.com/water**

7 Ways Alkaline Ionised Water Helps You Stay Healthy!

01. Weight Loss

02. Detoxification

03. Bone Health

04. Cellular Hydration

05. Heart Health

06. Energy/Endurance/Recovery

The list truly is endless. Check out **www.RethinkPlanner.com/water** as there is loads of great information there for you.

HERE'S TO YOUR HEALTH & WELLBEING!

You can have all the success, money and power that this world has to offer but it is worth nothing if you don't have inner peace, purpose and fulfilment.

Only by taking care of the inner dimension will you ever experience true joy, happiness and achievement from all your efforts expended in the material dimension.

HEALEXUS is a technology that allows you to go deep into that part of your iceberg that is below the waterline. When you are able to understand, work with, change and utilize this portion of your operating system, through connection with your Spiritual essence as it is sometimes called, you are able to change all aspects of your life.

What can HEALEXUS help me with?
Your default settings and subconscious thoughts

HEALEXUS technology helps you quickly cleanse your human energy fields so that you feel:

- Peace of mind
- Courageous
- Confident
- Focused
- Lighter
- Connected to nature
- Energised

For more information please visit
www.RethinkPlanner.com/healexus

Notes

Notes

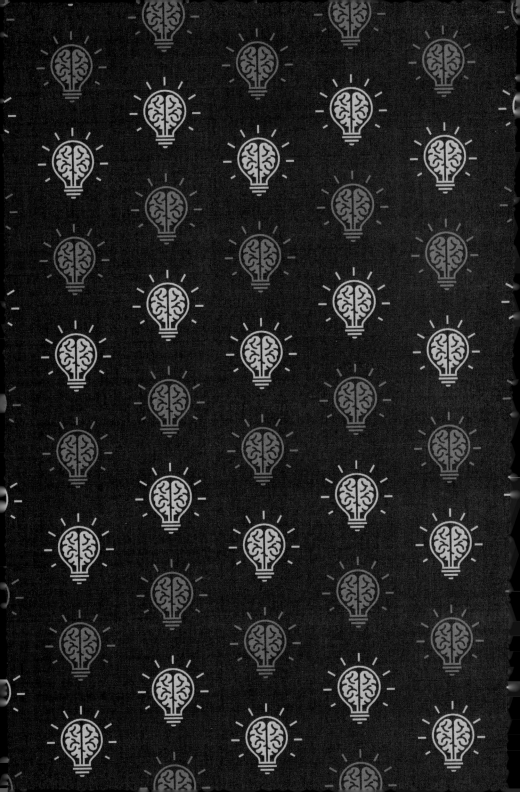